Life IN THE H⬤⬤D

MY STORY, GOD'S GLORY

Carla Person-McCray

Book Cover Design: Prize Publishing House

Printed by Prize Publishing House, LLC in the United States of America.

First printing edition 2024.

Prize Publishing House
P.O. Box 9856, Chesapeake, VA 23321
www.PrizePublishingHouse.com

Library of Congress Control Number: 2024925945

ISBN (Paperback): 979-8-9908345-8-3
ISBN (E-Book): 979-8-9908345-9-0

"This is a very good book. It kept my attention to the end. It made me smile, laugh, and tear up at times. This book is about the author's life and she does a very good job telling the story. If you want to read a book that gives you a little of everything, please read this book. You won't be disappointed."
- Jennifer Shepherd

"This book is awesome; it is must-read. It gives drama but is very authentic and raw. The author shares her life story unapologetically with no self-pity. I love this book, and it has helped me in so many ways. Thank you, Carla, for your honesty and authenticity. I pray that this book will help millions of people and be a #1 Best Seller."
- Jay Marie

"What an amazing read! I recommend this as a must-read! The book is very relatable, entertaining, suspenseful, and hopeful. It shows that even through the hard times, God is there! It is a true indicator that God is the author and finisher of our faith if we only trust in Him."
- K. Hickson

CONTENTS

INTRODUCTION

Philippians 4:6 says, "Be careful for nothing; but in every-thing by prayer and supplication with thanksgiving let your requests be made known unto God."

Every little girl has a dream of how she wants her life to be, from her husband to the wedding, how many children she wants, where she's going to live, and so forth. We pray and ask God for certain things in a man; God hears our request. He says, "Okay, I got you." However, we must remember that God's timing is not our timing, and when we see time passing, we get a little impatient and anxious.

We even tell God we want a man like our father. While some little girls see their fathers as heroes, some mothers do not talk about how their children's father is. Some fathers may be liars, cheaters, drug addicts, or whatever the case may be. We only see the surface. We really don't know what's deep down inside. So, when we ask God to send us a man like our father, and He does just that, we are mad at God. So, we have to be careful about what we are asking God for.

This book is to teach you to wait on God and to help you trust the process and stick to the plan God has set for you. As stated in Proverbs 3:6, "In all thy ways acknowledge Him, and he shall direct thy paths."

— chapter —

1

THE CHURCH

I grew up in a loving home with God-fearing parents and 11 siblings. My father was a pastor at a small church in College Park, Georgia. In 1989, on Christmas Eve, our house caught fire; we had nowhere to go, so we moved into my father's church while he and others rebuilt our house.

My father ran into some issues, so we could no longer live in the church. He worked for the city of East Point sanitation department, so when he finished his job, he came home and worked on our house. Many people came and helped my father and gave him materials to build. Our house was halfway finished when we moved in.

My father lost his church due to some other issues. After hearing that my father had lost his church, a bishop came and offered my father a church. So, my family and I worshipped there. It was only us. We were members, saints, and friends. So, my father decided we would just go and worship with the bishop and his church. We started going to this church. I think I was about 18 or 19 years old. I loved this church; the members were so nice and friendly, and I started making new friends.

When you are young, you don't know all the details of what's going on. This church had real live drama, like a soap opera. Now, there was this girl named Nicole. Nicole was dating the bishop's son, and he was the drummer of the church. Nicole loved this guy. He not only played the drums but also played with women's hearts. He would be with Nicole, then leave her, and start talking to this girl named Jada, both in the same church. Y'all, this was not a big church, so they knew each other. Jada loved him also. So, these young ladies would be arguing and fussing in the church; I had never seen anything like this in my life. Well, let me say, in the church.

After church, I would always hang out with Nicole, her sister, and the drummer's sister, the bishop's daughter. We were always together, going places and having fun. Mind you, I had just started attending this church, so I never really got to know Jada and her family. One day, Nicole, her sister, the bishop's daughter, and I came into the church. They all went into the back of the church where the kitchen was; I stayed in the front of the church in the sanctuary. Jada and her family were also in the sanctuary.

Jada's mother approaches me and says, "I know you are hanging out with them, and they may have told you some things about us." She says, "You get to know us for yourself, and don't let anyone put things in your head."

I said, "Yes, ma'am."

So now I have to try to figure out how I am going to stay friends with Nicole and them and start being friends with Jada and the others. I can't remember how it happened, but oh, it happened. When I got to know Jada and her family, I found that they were fun people to be around. Jada was silly; we could just look at each other and just start laughing. I'm glad her mother approached me because Jada and I have become really good friends.

We continued to go to the church for a while. Eventually, my family left because my mom was not pleased with the things that were going on in that church. I was around 20 now, so I could make my own decision. I stayed, I had friends there now. My mother was not happy with that decision, but there wasn't anything she could say. When I went to church and saw things happening, I would come home and share them with my siblings. This was some hot tea, y'all.

One day, my mom overheard me telling my sisters what was going on in the church. She waited for a while; then she called my name. She said, "I don't want you to go back over there."

I was so mad. I was not happy about this. I said, "Yes, ma'am."

See, when you are young and have never experienced stuff like this happening in the church, it excites you, but people, such as my mom, don't play about these things.

Jada and her family moved closer to me; we stayed three

doors down from each other; they were still going to the bishop's church. So, guess what, y'all? I was still getting the tea. All this made Jada and I become best friends.

Eventually, Jada and her family also left the church, so we all ended up at the old church my father pastored back in College Park, Georgia, under a new pastor, Pastor Willie Robinson.

2

CHOOSE ONE

ada and I did everything together, like going to see a movie and getting our hair and nails done when we could because Jada had a son, and I was always working. I basically lived with them. She and her sister would be outside when I got off work, so I would see them and go over there. We would talk and laugh, just having fun. Before you knew it, time had passed. So, I would just stay the night over at their house.

Years passed. Jada and her family moved to the other side of Atlanta. I was really sad about this, but we still stayed in touch over the phone. I didn't get to see them that much. Now that they were gone, I just worked even more because I needed money to get me a car.

One night, when I had just got off work, Jada called me. She said that she was pregnant by a guy named Anthony and that he wasn't claiming her baby. I told her not to worry about that. I told her that I would send her some money to help her with the baby. She said okay. She gave birth to a baby boy.

I worked for Wendy's ever since I was 16. I was only 22 years old when I was a trainee about to become a manager when this guy came in with his security uniform on, looking all nice and clean-shaven. He had a beautiful smile, and when I saw him, I got chills. I had never seen this guy before. When it was time to take his order, I couldn't because I was so nervous, but I finally got through it.

He looked around the counter, and he saw my sister, Melinda. He started talking to her. I was just looking. When he left, I immediately asked her who he was. She said that he was her husband's childhood best friend. I told her that he was nice-looking. We both started laughing. I don't know what made me start lusting after this man, but I did. I was not in the spirit. I was in the flesh, and that flesh needed to be crucified. Help, Lord!!

At my job, we used to get robbed all the time. So, they would give the police officers free meals if they sat down, and it was half-price if they left. So, we had police officers come in and out. Many of the officers would try their best to take me out on a date, but I would say no. I don't know what it was; I just wanted that guy. It was something about him. He must have known that I liked him because he started coming every day when there were plenty of other restaurants on that street.

After coming in day after day, he introduced himself.

He said his name was Ant, and he wanted to take me out on a date. I said yes. I was so happy. We began to date. He started introducing me to his friends. Three months into our relationship, we had sex, and I was barely going to church. I just wanted to be with him because I thought I was in love.

Ladies, this is the first mistake we make when we get a new man: we leave God. We must not lose sight of God because, without Him, we are lost. He is our road map. How do we think we are going to navigate through life without Him? Every time we went on a date, he would just pick me up from my house, and we would just leave. Ladies, we have to remember morals, such as a man coming knocking on the door and waiting on the inside for us. We have made it so easy for them just to call or text and say I'm outside.

I had just got off work. He called and said he was going to come and pick me up. I got into the shower and started getting ready, but when he came, I was still getting dressed, so he had to come in. He came in and sat down. He saw my photo book on the table and picked it up. He started looking through it. He stopped and began to laugh, so I asked him what he was laughing at.

He asked, "What is the girl's name?"

I was about to tell him. He said, "No, let me tell you her name. Her name is Jada."

I looked and said, "How do you know her?"

He said, "Look at this baby." It was a picture of her new son. He asked me if he looked like him.

I didn't say anything because I was shocked. After all, this was my best friend's baby's father. All kinds of things were going through my head. I was looking like this is truly a small world, and am I dreaming?

He picked up my house phone; yeah, y'all remember those house phones? He blocked out my number and called her. He told her that they both had a mutual friend. He had her on the speakerphone so I could hear her. She says, "Who?"

He said, "Carla."

She asked him how he knew me and if we were dating. He laughed. She hung up the phone in his face.

It wasn't even a minute before I saw her name on the caller ID. I was like, *Oh Lord! I don't know why he called her. I* was not ready to tell her this over the phone. But I knew I was going to have to tell her sooner or later. It looked like it was going to be sooner, so I picked up the phone.

She said, "Hey, what are you doing?"

I said, "Getting ready to go out."

She said, "Okay, call me when you get back."

I said, "Okay."

I already knew what she wanted, so when I got back home, I waited for a while. Then I called her. She made a lot of small talk. Then she gave the phone to her brother. He said, "Hey, how are you?"

I said, "Fine."

Then he asked me if I was dating someone. I asked him, "Why?" But I knew what this was leading up to.

He said, "Because I wanted to take you out."

I said no, I didn't have time. So, he handed her the phone back.

She says, "Guess who called me today?"

I was like, "Who?" As if I didn't already know.

She said, "Anthony, my baby's father."

I was like, "Really?"

She said, "Yeah. He told me he knew you."

I was like, "Yeah."

She said, "How do you know him?"

At this point, I paused and put the phone down. Tears rolled down my face. I could hear her saying hello. I was like, "Yeah, I'm here, trying to get myself together."

I already knew either way I told her, it was going to hurt because the damage was already done. And at this point, what was I supposed to do? I had to decide whether to choose my best friend or my boyfriend. Both of whom I loved.

She said, "So, what's up? Are y'all together?"

I said, "Yes."

She was like, "Oh really? That's what's up," and hung up the phone. I could tell she was mad.

I had no idea that this was her baby's father. But 99.9% of the time, we choose the man over the friend.

— chapter —

3

IGNORING SIGNS
AND RED FLAGS

Anthony and I continued to date, and we hung out more and more. I had already met some of his friends. Now, he started taking me around to meet his family. Meeting people's families is huge. So, I thought, *yeah, he wanted to be with me*. Ant had a daughter who was around six or seven when we got together. I met his mom and brother first. He had two friends who were running a hotel. He called his sister and told her to come and meet me. So, she came to the hotel. She tried to be cordial, but you can tell in your spirit when someone is not feeling you.

My family, on the other hand, are close. We try to get along with everybody. We talked about everything, so I was excited to tell my family about him. Mind you, one of my sisters already knew him, so that was a plus. One day,

I went to my mother's house, and I saw my sister, Sheila. I told her everything that was going on. I mean the good, the bad, and the ugly. I told her he had one child and maybe a second one by Jada.

I wasn't ready for what she was about to say. She said, "Girl, you are young and beautiful. You don't need to play stepmom to anybody; make your own family. Being a stepmom comes with a lot of drama. Pray about it and ask God." Y'all, this was the last thing you want to hear from your sister, especially when you feel like you are in love with someone. But you know, it's something about when you are in your early 20s; I don't know what it is about that age. You think you know everything and don't know anything. Child, I let that go in one ear and out the other.

I already knew that she was right. Even before I got with him, I prayed and asked God for a man who had no kids, was nice-looking, was in the church, and honored and respected God and me. They used to tell us in church, don't just tell God you want a man; put it in detail. So, I let my request be made known unto God.

God is the carpenter. When we make the request, He draws up the blueprint. He designs the house like we want it, and then He builds our house. When He builds it, it's already built, but here we come, trying to go behind Him and add on and take off.

Now, all that went out the door. All I was thinking was that God could save him and change his life. All kinds of crazy things were playing in my head just to make things right. My sister offended me badly. I was like, *honey, people always want to tell you to pray about something.* I was like, *did she pray about her husband...Whom she had been married to for about 10 or 15 years at the time.* I was like, *NO, she probably didn't. I don't think so. God made it work for her. He can do it for me.*

Everything seemed like it was happening so fast. Ant and I were hanging out so much, to the point that when I got home, it was late, and we both were tired. I even spent the night at his house sometimes.

One night, I came in late. I was staying with my sister, Lisa. She was married to Tommy. When I came in, I made a lot of noise because it was dark, and I was bumping into things. I wanted to shower, but I just didn't want to wake anybody up. I didn't know I already had. So, I just laid down and went to sleep. I woke up, jumped into the shower, and got ready for work. My sister called my name. She said, "When you get off, come straight home." They wanted to talk to me.

I was like, "Okay."

So, when I got off work, I went straight home. My sister and brother-in-law were in the kitchen. Now, one thing I loved about my sister's house was that whether you wanted to or not, good or bad, we were going to talk about the issues. My brother-in-law says, "What's up with you coming in, in the wee wee hours of the morning, and making all that noise?"

I always got offended no matter what and went straight

to defense mode. I said, "I wasn't trying to make any noise; I tripped on something, and that's what you heard. I didn't know I had a curfew, being that I am 24."

My brother-in-law was like, "You don't have a curfew. But I work. And this is my house. I need to make sure everything is safe and secure."

They could tell I had an attitude. My sister Lisa said, "You don't need to be out that late." She always had a way to tell you off with a scripture to back her up. She said, "You don't need to let your good be evil spoken of." I was looking at her from the side and rolled my eyes.

Tommy was such a gentleman and always knew how to defuse a fire. He said, "And if this is your boyfriend, why haven't you brought him in to meet us?" But after what my sister, Sheila, said, I didn't want him to meet anyone else. Tommy said, "Here's what you do; you call him, y'all pick a day when he can come and meet us; I want to take y'all out to eat and pay for everything." This made me so happy. I was no longer mad at my brother-in-law, but I was still mad at my sister. I was very sensitive, and everything hurt my feelings. I called him and told him everything they said. He agreed to come and meet them.

Maybe two or three weeks later, I moved out of my sister's house and moved in with Ant. So now I thought I was doing some grown-up things, and everything seemed to be going well. But they say you never know a person until you live with them. I have found this to be true.

It was around one or two in the morning. Ant gets a

phone call, so he gets out of bed, goes into the bathroom, and answers the phone. I was playing like I was asleep. He was talking to some woman. When I made some kind of noise, he would flush the toilet as though he was using it. Then he would come back to bed like nothing happened.

When you feel like you are in love with a person, you are blinded by all the signs and red flags that are being thrown on the play. The Bible says warning comes before destruction. Which means God warns us to get our lives right. But I also use this scripture in my personal life. We must be careful not to miss what God is trying to warn us about in our relationships.

4

THE DNA TEST RESULTS

It had been a while since we heard from Jada, so I knew she was mad at me. One day, we had just gotten off work. We headed home; Ant went to the mailbox. He had gotten summoned to come to court. Jada was seeking child support.

The day before he had to go to court, he wanted me to take off work and come with him to court. I didn't want to see Jada, so I said you can just go by yourself. He got mad and said we are supposed to be in a relationship, and we are supposed to support each other. I really wasn't trying to hear that. I didn't know how she was going to react seeing both of us together. I was not trying to get into a confrontation down there at the courthouse. I went to work. He was mad, but he got over it. Of course, when he got to court, they made him take a DNA test. So now he has to wait for the results to come in the mail.

Mind you, Jada, her family, and my family all still attended the same church. So, everyone at this church knew our business. This is what happens when you go to a small church; you can't hide anything because everyone is basically family, whether blood or not.

I just stopped going because I already had to go through drama. Now, I had to go through embarrassment, rumors, lies, and whispers. And like they say, there are two sides to every story, but if you only have one side of the story, that's what you will believe.

Some of my cousins would call me and tell me what Jada would be saying. So, one day, they called me and told me she said no matter where she saw me, it was "on-site." Now, I don't know if that was true or not, but everyone who knows me knows that I don't like confrontation, but I'm not backing down from a challenge.

One day, I got a call from one of my cousins who attended this church. She said they're having a revival, and she would like it if I attended. I asked her who was running the revival. She said Bishop Preston. Now, Bishop Preston was Jada's family good friend. So that should have given me a warning then just to say no. But all that was playing in my head was "on-site, on-site," over and over. I knew that this was nothing but the devil's plan, and I was about to let him use me.

I got off work, and like always, before we went into the house, we checked the mailbox. Ant got the mail. He received the paper from the court. His DNA test results came. Come to find out, her son was his son. So, we went into the house, and we talked about it. After talking about what we planned to do, I needed a breath of fresh air. So, I told him that I was going to the revival. He was not pleased with this. He said, "It's already late." One thing about Ant was that he did not like for me to drive, pump gas, or really do anything by myself at night.

I got into my car and drove to the church. When I got there, the bishop was already up and about to start praying for people. When I came in, it seemed like all eyes were on me; I really did not care. When church was over, I stayed and said my goodbyes to my family. As I was about to leave the church, the bishop of the night asked me if I was coming to church tomorrow. I told him I did not know. He said, "Come back because God has a word for you."

The next day, I got ready early so I could enjoy church since I hadn't been in a while. Little did I know that I was in for a treat. They put the bishop up. He read his scriptures and said, "If I used a topic, it would be, 'Turn Your Lights On.'" I remember this sermon like it was yesterday. He said, "Now, if you know you have stepped out of the will of God, turn your lights on." So, every time he said something, he told us he wanted us to say, turn your lights on.

Now, I don't remember everything he said word for word. I just remembered the part when he started preaching about me. He said, "Now, if you know that your best friend got a baby from your boyfriend."

Everybody said, "Turn your lights on."

After everybody said, turn your lights on, they said amen. Child, I had the devil in me. I stood up and shouted amen, too.

If only y'all could have seen my sister Sheila's face; she looked at the bishop with the meanest face she could give someone. You know that saying, if looks could kill, he would have been dead. She stood there staring at that man for a good while. She was letting him know, don't play with my sister. When he finished his sermon, he started an altar call. He called me up, which I already knew was going to happen.

He said, "I'm not going to embarrass you."

In my head, I'm like, *too late; you already have.* So, at this point, he's looking at me. I'm looking at him. He said, "You know what you are supposed to be doing. Don't let no man hinder you from doing what God wants you to do."

I was looking at him like, *child, please,* and some more stuff was going through my head. I kept it in my head because I was taught not to put my mouth on the preacher. I never liked it when people used the pulpit or God's name when they knew about your business.

Now church was over, and I was about to leave. I walked down to my car, and one of the members called my name, so I looked to see who it was; it was Janice. She said, "Jada wants you."

I said, "She wants who? I just passed her." But it wasn't like I didn't already know what she wanted, so I closed my car door and walked over to her.

She said, "I don't know if Anthony told you, but our results came in the mail. So now he has a son."

I was like, "Yeah, he told me, but that really doesn't have anything to do with me. That's something that he has to deal with."

She said, "I know. I was just letting you know."

I said, "Okay, thank you." So, I got in my car and drove to my mother's house.

While I was there, my sisters and I were talking about what happened tonight. After we finished talking, my oldest sister, Angela, wanted to go to the store. I told her I was going with her. Now, my mother stayed right behind the church. So, we could see the church when we drove by. When we drove by the church, Jada, her mom, her sister, the bishop, his wife, and my cousin, who had invited me, were outside, still talking at the church. Everyone else was gone. I told my sister to drive slowly. She drove slowly; I rolled the window down and hollered turn your lights on. My sister was like, "Girl." She couldn't get it out. She drove that car so fast. When we got back, they were gone.

— chapter —

5

THE CALLS

Now that he knew he had a son, they had to figure out how they were going to co-parent. So, of course, you know they had to talk on the phone with each other. Sometimes, when she called, he would have her on the speakerphone so I could hear what they were saying. I'm not going to lie. Sometimes, this made me jealous.

If y'all thought we had problems, then it really started to get crazy. Now, I'm not saying we didn't have any good times, but it seemed like the bad outweighed the good. It seemed like she knew that I was jealous because the calls were back-to-back; sometimes, she would call and just hand the baby the phone. Now, y'all know that when you are a baby, as he was, you don't want to be on the phone and don't want to talk. He was too busy trying to play. I could hear her calling his name, and he would be crying because he wanted to play.

The calls had gotten so bad that she was calling late at night. One night, she called late. Ant got up and went into his favorite place, the bathroom, because I was going off. I was like, "There is no way y'all got to talk this late at night." She could hear me in the background. I guess she was asking him what I was saying. He was trying to shut me up, telling me to be quiet. I did not realize that there was not a specific time when a kid got sick or things of that nature because I did not have kids of my own.

So, when he got off the phone, he told me the baby was sick, and she might have to take him to the hospital because he had a fever, and it was high. Y'all don't know how small I felt, just running my mouth, but this was just one night. She still called late at night when the baby should have been asleep. I would get in bed and just cry sometimes. It seemed like she had the upper hand, and there was nothing I could do about it. One night, I got in bed, and I prayed to God. I said, "Lord, I see how Sarah felt when Hagar had Ishmael. Lord, are you punishing me for not being in the church anymore? Lord, what's up?" God began to tell me He was making me.

Child! Who wants to hear this when you are going through it? I'm like, *making me into what?* God is quiet now. I'm like, *Lord, where are you? Speak to me.* Tears rushing down my face. I'm trying not to sniff because I didn't want Anthony to hear me, but he could hear me. He asked me what was wrong. I would just say nothing.

— *chapter* —

6

THE FIGHTS

E ver since the results, it seemed like Anthony and I fussed every single day. Sometimes, it seemed like he was just trying to pick a fight. We only had one car, so we did everything together. We needed a little break from each other for a couple of hours even though we had breaks when we both went to work.

Now, I told y'all that Anthony's sister, Shanell, wasn't feeling me. To this day, I still don't have a clue why. But as we used to say, it is what it is. She liked his daughter's mother and Jada. She really didn't know me and did not give me a chance. Anthony and Shanell would talk on the phone sometimes. They were not really close. She got on his nerves sometimes. Most of the time, when she called, she needed to borrow money or something. Just because she didn't like me and we had a joint account, I would be in the background saying no, no, no, and no. This made her mad. Anthony would just say we don't have it. Sometimes that was true, and sometimes it wasn't. He gave it to her sometimes.

The fussing continued; it seemed like I just could not catch a break. I was fussing with him, Jada, and his sister. I would get so mad at him because it seemed like I was fighting battles by myself. I used to tell him, "You just let people talk to me any kind of way. You never have my back." All I wanted him to do was fight for me and not me to fight over him. Have you ever been in a fight? Or you are about to fight, and everybody is cheering you on, telling you I got your back, but when it's time to fight, they are nowhere to be found.

Anthony was not a bad guy; he just wasn't for me. And when you go on your will and with your plan, you go through some things. God had to let the whale swallow me, just like He did Jonah. God made it uncomfortable for me. There were sleepless, crying, and lonely nights.

Do you know that you can be with someone and still be lonely? The way things were going, it seemed like I was in a dream or a fairytale, just as in the fairytale Cinderella and her wicked stepsisters. I was trying hard to make it work. But that shoe just didn't fit me. Just as the wicked stepsisters did, they tried to force it to go on. One of them even got it on, but it hurt and hurt until she just wanted to scream. It was time. I just wanted to scream, y'all, but I just tried to endure the pain. I just wasn't ready to take the shoe off. There wasn't anything that tied us together. We had no kids together, and we were not married. I just wouldn't take the shoe off.

— *chapter* —

7

BABY NUMBER TWO

t seemed like our relationship was just hitting rock bottom by the hour, but he and Jada were getting more and more acquainted. He told me that she had enrolled in the Job Corps. In my head, I was like, *what did this have to do with the price of tea in China? What brought on this conversation? What does this have to do with your son?* But I held my peace because I wasn't in the mood for an argument.

I started seeing changes in our normal routine. Now, mind you, we only had one car, but it was my car. My brother-in-law, Tommy, helped me get it while I stayed with him. Ant now wanted to drop me off at work so he could keep the car. He made an excuse that they were slow at his job. I didn't see any harm in that.

One day, my sister, Robin, called me. She asked me if I knew that Jada was pregnant. I said, "No. Anthony did not mention that."

27

She said, "Jada's mom and I were talking. She was insinuating that the baby was Ant's."

I said to my sister, "Girl. Please. We are together too much. Don't you think if that were true, Jada would have rubbed that in my face?"

My sister was like, "Alright."

My sister had a way of saying something without saying it if you know what I mean. That alright meant look into it. I said, "I will ask him." Y'all, I was so naïve about many things. All I knew was work and church. I would give people the benefit of the doubt. Now, was I ready to ask him about this? No.

You know how you wash dishes, and you put all the dishes in the sink. Those of you who still wash dishes can relate. Then, when it comes to the knives, spoons, and forks, it seems like you will never finish them. You reach carefully into the sink because you have knives in there. So, you grab a handful, and you wash them. You reach in there again and grab another handful. So now you think you are finished. You put your hands in there to see if you got them all. Seems like you got them all, but when you let the water out, you see a knife, spoon, or something. Y'all, this is how my life was. It just felt like no end. You get over one hill, and here comes a mountain. You climb the mountain, and here comes a valley. Just on and on. I was like, *Lord, how much more do I need to be made?*

When he got home, I asked him about it. He said he knew that she was pregnant. So, in my head, I was like, *oh really? You are sitting up here talking about how she entered Job Corps but couldn't tell me this; oh, ok.* But he said that the baby wasn't his. So, I was like, *okay.* Something in the water was just not right. But I still gave him the benefit of the doubt because she had already taken him to court one time for a DNA test, so he already knew what he was up against. And besides, she didn't say anything about it, so I believed him.

Months passed, and Jada was due to have her baby. This was the same time that Ant mysteriously had to go out of town for something, and I can't remember what it was for.

— *chapter* —

8

I'M PREGNANT NOW

I used to love my job because the people I used to work with made it fun. Every time my friend Neka and I worked, all we did was laugh. Work is where I found peace. No one ever knew what Anthony and I were going through because I always came in with a smile and was ready to work. Some of my co-workers thought we were this perfect couple. Some of them would even say, "There goes my favorite couple," and we would just smile.

Then, I started not to like going to work. I didn't like the smell of grease, so every time I smelt it, I would run into the bathroom and throw up. My friend, Neka, said, "Genie," that's what she used to call me, "You need to go to CVS or somewhere and get a pregnancy test."

I was like, "Girl, I'm not pregnant; I still have cycles."

She said, "You can have cycles and still be pregnant."

This was news to me. This was the first time I heard this. So, I said, "Okay."

When I got off work, I went to CVS, as she said, and got the pregnancy test. When I got home, I was there by myself. I wasn't going to tell Anthony until I knew for sure. I followed the instructions on the box. When I looked at the applicator, it said not pregnant; this was no lie; I was disappointed. I thought for sure I was. I was all over the place because my motive for wanting a baby was all wrong. I thought having this baby was going to help our relationship and bring us back closer. I also wanted this baby to make Jada mad. Child, I was just foolish. Thank God for growth.

I threw the applicator in the bathroom trash. Ant came home; I was lying in bed. He said, "Hi."

I gave him one of those dry hi's.

He was like, "What's wrong with you?"

I said, "Nothing." So, he gets up and goes into the bathroom. I think this was his favorite spot because this is where I think he found peace. Lord knows if something was not right, he was going to know it. Somehow, he saw the applicator in the trash, got it out, and said, "So you thought you were pregnant?"

I said, "I just get sick now when I go to work."

He said, "So this is what you are mad about?"

I said, "I'm not mad."

He says, "You look like it."

I said, "I just don't feel good."

He was like, "Oh, okay."

But Lord knows I wanted a baby.

At this point, I had to talk to God. It's funny how we only want to talk to God when we need Him because I know I wasn't talking to Him every day. I said, "Lord, why didn't you give me a baby? Cause right now, we are looking like Leah and Rachel." I told y'all this is all I knew: church and work.

I got to work; my friend asked me if I had taken the test. I said, "Yes."

She could see the disappointment all over my face. She said, "Friend, God will give you a baby."

Tears began to roll down my face. Yes, they call me a crybaby, but still, all in all, I needed to figure out why I was getting sick when I came to work. I took the next day off. I called my sister, Melinda, and asked her if she could go to the clinic with me; she said okay.

I was at my mom's house, so when she pulled up, my mother was outside. She was so happy to see my sister. She asked her what she was doing over there so early. My sister said, "I'm taking Carla to the clinic."

My mom was like, "For what?"

My sister said, "To see what's wrong with her."

We got to the clinic, and they asked me when my last cycle was. I told her. The nurse said, "We may have to give you a pregnancy test."

I told her I had already taken one at home. She said we will just give you another to see. So, she gave me a home test first, and she said it was defective.

The nurse said, "See, a lot of people think when you drink water, it helps you to use the bathroom. It does, but it also dilutes your urine, and sometimes, it makes the test inaccurate."

I was like, "Wow."

She said, "I need to draw your blood." She drew my blood, came back, and said, "Congratulations, you are pregnant."

Y'all, oh, the joy that flooded my soul; something happened, and now I know He touched me and made me whole. My motive was still all wrong. Just messy, as the young people would say. I got home. I told Ant. I think he was happy; I can't remember. All that mattered was that I was.

— chapter —

9

TRUTH REVEALS

One day, I went to pick Anthony up from work, and when he got in the car, he said he wanted me to take him over to Shanell's house. I rolled my eyes and said, "Why do you want to go over there?" Shanell didn't stay around the corner; she lived like 20 or 30 minutes away.

He said, "I just need to get away."

This made me so mad, but I said, "Okay."

He did this for about two weeks straight so he could get a so-called break. Not realizing that what you do in the dark will come to the light. And this is what it certainly did, came to light.

He was going down there because Jada moved in with Shanell. Of all the places she could have gone, I thought, *here, really?* Ant said her mama put her out, so she had no-where to go. In my head, I thought *Shanell would do some junk like this to get back at me.*

Now, I know y'all are wondering how I found this out, so here it is. Shanell calls Anthony. Now, she doesn't have an inside voice, so you can hear her without her being on the speaker phone. In the background, you can hear the baby crying. One thing about Ant is that he does not like a lot going on in your background, so he tries to be slick and turn the phone down. He is yelling at her like he can't hear her. At this point, I'm ear-hustling. Shanell said Jada is doing something. I don't even know what she said she was doing; all I heard was Jada.

I was just ready for him to get off the phone so I could go straight into police mode. You know how they have you in that room, asking all kinds of questions? Let the interrogation begin. I'm not trying to play all innocent. I used to go off at the drop of a dime. I did not care.

Being with the wrong person is like getting your packages delivered to the wrong address. You know you ordered something, and you need it that day. You see, it says delivered, so when you go outside to get it, it's not there. You are frustrated, aggravated, and irritated, like a ticking time bomb. I needed Anthony to love me; I wanted his love. I longed for his love, but God made him look elsewhere. Sometimes, they don't really know why they do the things that they do. We always say that's the devil; no, that's God, letting us know we're at the wrong house. It looks like your house, check the address.

So, now that Jada is there with Shanell, this brings on insecurities in me, and plus, I'm pregnant, so my emotions are all over the place. I think they are going to be down there talking about me. All kinds of things. But I just could not let them think they got the best of me. This is the type of game we play in our life. I just couldn't let them win. Even if it caused me stress and pain, they were not going to win.

Ladies, this is sad; we torture ourselves just to say we won. This was no longer about him; this was war. They were not going to make me give up and look bad as if I wasn't already looking that way.

One day, it was about 5:00; it was time for me to get off. I did not call Anthony to pick me up because I was going to buy a perm from the beauty supply store. Yeah, y'all know about perms, Hawaiian silk. I had to keep my hair right.

Child, I got in line; it was time for me to pay. I gave her my card, and it said declined. She said, "Your card declined; you don't have any money."

I'm like, "Yes, I do." I'm telling her to try it again.

She tries again and says, "Nope, no money."

Y'all, the perm was only like five-something back then, so this was really embarrassing. I got out of the line and called Ant. He said, "Oh yeah, I let Shanell borrow some money. She was short on her light bill."

I was so mad; I was like, "If you don't go and get my money, I know something." But Shanell had already paid the bill with it.

He kept apologizing, talking about how he was going to

pay me back. Shanell had convinced him that since his kids were there, he needed to help her with the bills.

I said, "No, he is not going to take care of two households." And he wasn't sure if the other baby was his.

— chapter —

10

LIES AND DECEIT

Jada must have had enough of Anthony's mess. She called me and said, "When you get off work, can we meet?"

I said, "Yes."

She said, "I wasn't going to tell you this, but it seems like Ant has been lying to both of us."

She said, "My baby girl, yes, she is his. All I asked him to do was give me money to take care of her, and he could not even do that." I was trying to hold back the tears. She said, "He keeps telling me he's going to leave you because he wants his family."

This really got to be one of the hardest things to hear, being that I am pregnant with his fourth child. In my head, I'm like, *Shanell must have put her up to this.* I wanted to blame everybody, but the person who was really to blame was Anthony. I didn't even want to see that picture. I still could not see that anything I did or tried wasn't going to make him love me the way I deserved to be loved.

Ladies, can I talk to you? Having a baby is not going to make a man love you; having sex with them, buying him everything he wants, cooking for him, hitting flips off the chandelier, nothing, and I say nothing is going to make a man love you if you are not his choice. Although he told me he loved me. Love is action. His actions showed something else, and I wasn't feeling his love.

So, Jada told me she was going to take him back to court, but she didn't know when. I knew right then that she was telling the truth.

I did not tell Anthony about this conversation because I wanted to see if he was really going to admit to it. He never said anything. Mind you, when he had to go to court the first time, he wanted me to go, but when he got his court papers this time, he did not want me to come. He was making up excuses for why I needed to go to work. He said we needed the money. So, he went to court, but they rescheduled. They still gave him a DNA test.

As women, we never stop to think or see the hurt of the other woman. She had two kids with Anthony, and he denied them both. Do you know how hurtful that is? But at that time, I did not care. One thing is for certain, and two things are for sure: that hurt people, will hurt people, and that's what we kept doing to each other.

Anthony has a cousin named Doug. Doug was a fun person to hang out with; He kept me laughing. One day, we were hanging out at our house, and Doug wanted to go see his friend. While at the house, Doug had been drinking, and when he drank, he was really funny, just saying whatever was in his head. You know how you get drunk and just start talking about everything under the sun?

Anthony had gone to court that morning, which I didn't know because, like I said, we only had one car, and he had dropped me off. He had his DNA test results but just wasn't saying anything, trying to hide it. We pulled up at Doug's friend's house. Doug is like, "Hey, cuz, how was court, and what were the test results?"

He was trying to be discreet and tell Doug to be quiet. I was looking at him, and I said, "Yeah, what were the test results?"

He did not say anything.

I said, "Well, there goes my answer."

Mind you, I am pregnant, so I am wobbling along. Love will make you do some crazy things. *Why was I walking? That was my car.* It was hot outside, so I was sweating like never before. Ant gets in the car and tries to come after me. I am so stubborn. I just kept wobbling along. He said, "I was going to tell you when we were alone." But it's funny how his cousin knew about the court and the results.

Now I know y'all are saying, well, I would have done this, and I would have done that, or I would have just left. Enough is enough. Everyone has played the fool before. You have old fools and young fools. I don't like to call people fools, but we all have done foolish things; I know y'all might be thinking I had daddy issues. No, my father was present in my life. He loved us. I wasn't seeking his attention, and he wasn't absent. He lived with us; I had a good relationship with my father. Because these are the kinds of things people will tell you when you're going through stuff like this.

Your flesh just wants what it wants. Everyone has an addiction. Whether it's drugs, alcohol, eating, lusting, lying, cheating, or whatever it may be. We look at drug addicts and say, why won't they just stop? They used to be so beautiful, now look at them or look at him/her they are too fat. Why don't they just stop eating? Everything is easier said than done, especially when you are not battling with these things.

chapter

11

MY BUNDLE OF JOY
IS COMING

No one in my family knew all this was going on because one thing about me: I like to prove people wrong. But how can you prove them wrong when they are right? I wasn't going to admit that.

After finding out the results, I went to stay with my sister, Melinda. I didn't tell her any of this. I told her it was getting close for me to having the baby, and Anthony had to work. He takes the car, so it would have been best if I stayed there so I wouldn't be by myself. She said it was okay. I know y'all are wondering why I didn't tell her about what was going on. Mind you, Anthony was already friends with her. So, I wasn't trying to get her involved.

At this point, I was so miserable. This is not how I pictured my pregnancy. My due date was on the 4th of July, which was also Anthony's birthday. I was always saying to him, I'm not going to be in nobody's hospital on the 4th of July. I wanted to be somewhere eating some ribs, chicken, macaroni, and stuff like that. He would just shake his head.

I was sitting on my sister's porch, looking pitiful. My sister's neighbor saw me. She said, "Girl, you look like you are tired and ready to pop."

I said, "I am."

She asked me when I was due, and I told her. This was like on June 30th. She said, "Are you ready to go in?"

I said, "Yes, ma'am."

She said, "You can do three things."

I was like, "Okay."

She said, "You can take some Castro Oil."

I was like, "That's out of the question."

"Or you can have sex."

I thought that was why I was in this predicament now.

"Or you can just walk up and down this street."

I was like, "That sounds more like it."

So, my niece, my nephew, and I walked up and down the street until we got tired. Later on that night, I was having contractions. The pain was coming and coming. I tried to go to sleep, but I just couldn't. I said a prayer until the pain subsided enough for me to go to sleep. Early in the morning, the pain increased to the point that I had to wake my sister up. She said, "Here." She gave me a notepad and a pencil. She said, "I want you to time your contractions."

At first, they were ten minutes apart. Then it went down

to eight minutes. It kept decreasing; by the time they got to five minutes, she said, "Let's go to the hospital."

My sister called my mother and Ant. Ant said he was going to meet us at the hospital. My sister went to pick up my mom because she wanted to come. We pulled up at the hospital. We were talking with the nurse. The nurse said, "How far along are your contractions?"

I looked at my notepad and told her. She looked at my notepad and started laughing; she was like, "Aw, you got a little notepad." At this point, I really didn't see anything funny. When you are in pain, you don't find anything funny.

They put me in a wheelchair and strolled me over to the desk, where they asked me a million and one questions. When I tell y'all, I was the meanest pregnant person in the world. They kept asking questions. I said, "Look, I am not going nowhere; I am in pain. Can y'all please take me to a room and get me some medicine?"

The nurse says, "This is your first baby, honey; you could be here all night or maybe not. You can just be having Braxton Hicks."

In my head, I'm like, "Girl, I don't care about no Braxton Hicks or any other Braxton. Just give me some medicine. What is Braxton Hicks?"

She was like, "False contractions."

I knew I couldn't be having any false contractions because this pain was real.

Finally, she took me to the back, but not into a room. We were in a hallway where she wanted me to get out of the wheelchair and walk. I couldn't walk. I did all the walking that I could do yesterday. She said, "We only have one labor room, and they had to give that room to the person who is actually ready."

My sister said, "Carla, you are going to have to get up and walk."

I see my mother over in a chair, rocking back and forth, calling Jesus. So, I got up and walked. The pain was intense. I had to stop. I asked my sister, "Can you please tell them to check me?"

She said, "They will, but just keep walking; I know you're in pain, but you have to open your cervix."

I walked for about five minutes; I stopped and looked at my mom. I said, "Can y'all please tell them to check me?" It felt like the baby was coming. My sister went and found the nurse. The nurse didn't want to check me because she was so focused on this being my first baby. She checked me. When I tell y'all, I have never seen someone run so fast in a hospital like that in my life. She said, "You are six centimeters." Right when she checked me, my water broke.

While they were getting me prepared for delivery, Ant walked in the door. He started talking to my mom and sister. I asked the nurse if they were going to give me an epidural. She said, "Do you want one?"

I said, "Yes."

She said she was sorry, but it was too late. It was a blessing; I did not have to wait that long because the baby came fast. A few pushes, and she was out.

We got home; everybody wanted to see the baby. I had her on July 1st. I was out of the hospital by the 3rd. Shanell came by the house. Oh, I forgot to tell y'all that she was pregnant too. Her baby was due in September.

Shanell used to try and make small jokes and slick comments. She said, "Well, Ant, are you going to make Carla take a DNA test?" I looked at her and rolled my eyes. She said, "Girl, you know I'm just playing with you."

I named her Kayla. Kayla was only about two weeks old when Ant came in and asked me if I wanted any more kids. Now, y'all know if you just had a baby, and a man asks you if you want more kids, you are going to say no. I said, "No."

He said, "Well, good because I made an appointment to get a vasectomy." I'm looking like, *really?* He says, "You are going to have to drive me down there." I was not even really supposed to be outside. I got up and got the baby and me ready. He drove and got the procedure done.

— chapter —

12

JOBLESS

Things got really rough. Somehow, Ant lost his job. So, I'm the only one working. Well, let me say, he was doing security in our apartment complex, so that was a plus. We didn't have to pay rent, but all the other bills fell on me. At times, it was just overwhelming, to the point that I just sat in my car and cried, praying and asking God to help me. It was a time when I didn't know what to do. It was good that I worked at Wendy's, so we didn't have to worry about food. Plenty of times, I had to call my sister, Robin, to borrow money. She would always come through.

Ant was putting in job applications; it seemed like everywhere. No callbacks. He did little side hustle jobs, such as bounty hunting, just to help because we were sinking. And just because of my pride, stubbornness, and acting like everything was okay, I didn't want to ask for help.

One day, I sat in my car, weeping and praying because I

didn't know what to do. Yeah, I know I cry a lot. Once again, I said, "Lord, help me!!! Lord, why aren't you helping me? I need your help." I sat in my car in silence. About 15 minutes later, God said to go to Lisa's house.

It's funny how we ask God for help and still argue with Him.

I was like, "Lord, I don't want to go down there. You know we don't have any money; we need to save gas." Like He wasn't aware of all this.

So, I went into the house and told Ant. At first, he said the same thing I told God, such as we need to save gas, then he was like, "I'm going with you." We got in the car and drove to my sister's house. My sister and Tommy were in the kitchen. Tommy reached for Kayla. He loved babies. He loved to see her do this thing; when you look at her, she would turn her head to the side as though she was saying, "What are you looking at?" This made him laugh so hard.

My sister and I went into her room. One thing about us is that we knew when any of us just needed to talk. I had to let that pride spirit go if I wanted to get help. God sent me down there. I was telling her that I was overwhelmed. I said Ant had no job. She said to go ask Tommy if they had any openings at his job. So, I waited for a while; then I called Ant's name. I asked him to see if Tommy's job had any openings. I didn't want Ant to think that my sister and I were talking about him. He asked Tommy. Tommy was the Supervisor of a wine warehouse. Tommy told him to fill out an application, so he did.

One week passed with no answer. Two weeks passed, and still no answer. We kept going to my sister's house asking Tommy, but he would just say no openings yet. So, I got in my car and started praying. I said, "Lord, you told me to go down there, I went, so what did I go down there for?"

When we are desperate, we try to make God move on our time. God is like hold up; I am the director. I am running this show; you need to take two and check your line because you have gotten off the script.

God said, "Carla, trust me, have faith and be patient."

I'm like, "God, I trust You. I am patient, and I have faith." I don't know why I'm telling Him I got all this when He knew I didn't. Because He would not have told me to have it, and I wouldn't be worrying about it.

Around that third week. Tommy called Ant. There was an opening, and he said that he got the job. We went to their house to thank Tommy personally. We were so happy, especially me.

Years went by, and we moved into this house that we had taken over from my nephew and his girlfriend. After we moved in, there were a lot of problems with that house. The water was coming from this well in the backyard; this made our water bill go sky-high. The pipe burst, and we kept calling the landlord, but there was no answer. The water was all in our yard. Ant had to go and turn the water off. Mind you, we had a small baby. No water, no bath, no nothing. So, I'm mad; I called him again. I left messages on his answering machine, and I told him to bring us back our deposit, and we would just move. He called me back then; he was mad. I'm like, "What are you mad about?" He lived right up the street from us. I guess he didn't want to come because it was a Sunday. I didn't care about any of that. He came down there harassing us, telling us to move out of his house.

I had to go to work that night. I told my boss what was going on; I told her to give me a few hours, and I would try to come in. She let me know that I needed to come in because there wasn't another manager who could take my place; she said she had been there all day and was ready to go home. So, every hour on the hour, she called. I was irritated and aggravated by both of them. My boss said, "You need to get here now."

I said, "You know what? You can have this job; I already told you my situation." I was almost done. I couldn't finish because of all of her calls, so I quit.

— chapter —

13

THE ULTIMATUM

So, y'all, I'm still holding on. Now it's been about five years we have been together. Kayla was around one. It seemed like love was in the air. Many of our close friends were tying the knot. So, I asked him when we were going to get married. He said, "I love you, but I'm not ready for that." He said, "When I get married, I only want to get married one time."

Look, ladies, when a man says this, this is a sure sign that he is not trying to marry you. It doesn't take more than five years to realize if you want to spend the rest of your life with a person. Especially when you are doing all the things that married couples are doing anyway. All you need is the paper to back it up. My dad used to say, "Why does a man have to buy a cow when he can get the milk for free?" Didn't understand that saying then, but as I got older, it hit me differently.

I told him that I was about to start back going to church. I said, "I don't want to live like this anymore." I told him that I was going to move back with my mother.

Now it's getting to be like I'm pressuring him into marrying me. When a man loves you, he is in pursuit of you. He longs for you.

My cousin Terry Scott preached a message one Sunday; it stuck with me. He preached "In Pursuit of God." He said, "As the deer pants for the water, my soul longs for thee." He said that a deer sweats in his mouth and over his body. So, in one day, he loses about a gallon of water. If he doesn't get to the water, he will die.

It seemed like I lost my worth, my value, and my morals. This is why it's important not to lose yourself in a man. I have never been insecure about myself. Because like I said men wanted me. They were in pursuit of me. When I wasn't at work, they asked for me. But we want what we want. I was losing gallons of water by the day. I was spiritually dying but willing to sacrifice it all for what I thought was love.

Now, it's funny how I was willing to move back with my mother with a baby. But when there were no ties, I couldn't walk away.

He eventually got the ring. He told my sister, Melinda, that he was going to propose, and he was going to do it at the College Park reunion. Now, anybody who knows about these reunions knows there are so many people. Everybody and their mama are there. But those who know me know I don't like a lot of attention. I am really shy.

My sister knew this about me, so she told me this was what he was about to do. He wanted her to bring me to the top of Brady Gym, where they had the DJ. I was so glad my sister told me this. Because I was not going up there with all those people. He was so mad. Oh well.

Now I know y'all are saying my sister should not have done that, especially when I was the one who wanted to get married. Yes, this is true. But this is what I'm telling y'all: it is important that you learn your mate. We had been together for five years, and he didn't know me. He knew some things I liked and didn't like. For instance, he knew I did not like mayo. That's only because I instilled that in him. Every time we went somewhere, I would say that, so this was embedded in his head. For most of our relationship, we argued, so there wasn't that much time to get to learn with each other. He could have just done this with just my family and the people we knew. I didn't know all those people at that reunion. I would have had a fit.

Of course, he was mad and didn't want to propose now because he wanted to do it in front of everybody. He gave me the ring at home, and at this point, there wasn't a real proposal. See, these are the things we allow and settle for; he wanted it to be a scene and show for people. But we don't care how they give it to us as long as they do it.

We seek attention because we lack it. The things we go through so that people can congratulate us. We no longer do it for love. As Tina Turner said, "What's love got to do with it?"

I felt like I suffered. I went through it, and I endured pain and shame. So, I deserved this prize, this trophy. And I also wanted to let Jada see my prize, and for once, I would be the first. Do you see how foolish that sounds? God doesn't work like that. We want Him to bless us in our mess and stinky thinking. I was too busy trying to get one up on this girl. I couldn't figure out how to love this man properly, but I was ready to enter a marriage with him.

— *chapter* —

14

WE DO

Now we are engaged. I let Anthony know that I didn't want to be engaged for a long time. This is just another way for people to waste more time; I was just in a rush. What was I rushing for?

We don't seek God, or let me say I didn't. We didn't get any counseling; it was just out of order. I knew the word, so why didn't I consult God? Because in my head I already knew that he was not in the plan for my life. I was trying to change God's mind. I was too busy trying to help God. Not realizing that God didn't need my help. He needed me to go sit down somewhere.

Now, all this time I have been with Anthony, we had sex before marriage and a baby out of wedlock. All that's playing in my head is 1 Corinthians 7:9, "It is better to marry than to burn." Child, I don't even think I picked up my Bible half the time.

It was Kayla's 2nd birthday. I asked my sister Melinda if she could keep her for a few hours. We did not tell anybody that we were going to the courthouse to get married. I don't know what I was expecting, but this was not it. I don't know why I thought it was going to be me and him in the courtroom. There were like five or ten couples in there. They call your name; you go up there in front of the judge. You say your vowels, and then you kiss, and that's it. This is not how I pictured my wedding. There weren't any pictures, no family, no kind of memories. I guess all that mattered was that I was Carla Hood now.

We leave the courthouse. We are in downtown Atlanta, so y'all know how crazy the traffic was. Anthony was just walking across the street. There was no waiting on me; there was no holding my hand or anything. In my head, I'm like, *what is going on?* I'm like, *did we just get married? It didn't seem like it.* I was so mad. *This was supposed to be the happiest day of my life. Why am I mad on my wedding day?* The whole car ride was nothing but silence. We go pick up the baby. We told my sister. I, with my fake smile, acted like I was happy.

We stayed at my sister's house for a while. It got late, so we left and went home. Now Kayla was asleep. So, I got into the shower. I am crying. Why am I crying on my wedding night? Because I knew I made this bed, and now I had to lie down in it.

I get out of the shower and put on my night clothes. Ant wanted to have sex. I was not in the mood for that. Y'all, I was stubborn as a mule. I went to Kayla's room, closed the door, and just cried. Ant was so mad. I came back into the room and got in the bed. I was still mad. I didn't want him to touch me. We didn't even consummate our marriage.

We do things on our own and expect God to bless us. The signs were always there. We stood in that courtroom saying vows that we didn't really know the true meaning of.

We said, "What God has joined together let no man put asunder," and God is like, "Child, please, I had nothing to do with that."

There are so many marriages God had nothing to do with. We just forged His name. You remember when you were in school and got a bad grade on your report card. You didn't want them to see that grade, so you signed your parent's signature. This is what we are doing: signing God's name on our license. And you know what that means: our licenses are fake.

— *chapter* —

15

GOD WILL MEND

started going back to church more. I already knew I needed God, but like we always say, "I got to get it right." So, my becoming Mrs. Hood, I guess, was my way of making things right. But I did not understand that it had nothing to do with me and my name changing. None of that was making it right.

This is what you call playing God, not in a way that you're trying to be Him, but as though you want something from Him. Just as our children play us when they want something, they clean up without being asked, or they tell us they love us. We act like the Creator doesn't know our every move. But He is a great God and still blesses us despite our motives.

Things began to change for us. I convinced Ant to come to church, or more like forced him. Telling him he needed to come to church so that God could bless our marriage. There

I go again in the way, trying to help God. Like God didn't know how to get him in church. We must watch how we manipulate people into doing things we want them to do.

Anthony started coming to church more and even started driving the church van. Things were looking up for us. One night, we went to church. It was a revival. There was this prophet named Prophet Davis there. He said, "I want to pray for marriages," so all the married couples came up. He prayed for me and said, "God has anointed you to sing, and when you sing, chains will be broken." He said, "When things are going wrong, just sing, and things will change." So that's what I did; I sang day and night.

Things had changed for our good. Jada and I even mended our friendship. She even let her kids come and spend some weekends with us. We were co-parenting. Jada even got married and invited me to her wedding, which was absolutely beautiful. I was like, *now, this is how you get married.*

God was just mending all the relationships. Shanell and I started to talk more. It was as if God said, "This is it. You have gone through enough. It's harvest time."

I was happy He had mended Jada and my relationship. We would just talk and talk. Jada let me know that she was only letting her kids come over because of me. She still wasn't really talking to Anthony, which was fine with me. I really did love her kids. Kayla got to know her siblings. We both had matured and no longer wanted to hurt each other anymore.

— *chapter* —

16

LIVING WITH THE OTHER WOMAN

*Y*ears later, Anthony was still coming to church, but just not as much as he used to. Something seemed to be off. He started being distant. One day, I asked him if we could talk. I told him I was unhappy. I said you seem distant. And to make matters worse, our lease was up, and we had nowhere to go. He said he just had a lot on his mind. He said, "Ask your sister Lisa if you could move in with her, and I will just go to Jerome's house." Jerome was another one of his childhood friends. So, I said okay. He said we can work on our credit and get a house.

Now, throughout our relationship, we were never really stable. So, getting a house would be good for us. Kayla and I moved to my sister's house. We didn't get to see Anthony that much, but we talked every day.

It seemed strange that when I called around 7:00 or 8:00, he would never answer. So, I asked him about it. He said he was really tired. They had been working him over. Now, mind you, we shared the same account, so all that working over was not showing up in that account.

It was around my sister Melinda's birthday. Her birthday is August 29th, and my birthday is September 4th. Her husband and Ant would throw us this big barbecue cookout every year. My sister and I had already told them that we did not want to have a cookout this year. We wanted to do something different. They still did the cookout. So, my sister and I got into the car, and we left. I left Kayla with Anthony. They were trying to stop us, but we kept going. Anthony was so mad, but I did not care.

Listen when a person really loves you. They are going to do whatever makes you happy, especially on your birthday. Loving someone is not hard, nor even making them happy. When you are in love with a person, nothing excites you more than to see a smile on their face. It can just be bringing home their favorite snack. This lets them know they were on your mind. You know that saying, "It's the thought that counts." Well, I don't like that saying. Only because people think they can give you anything, and you're supposed to be happy with that.

For example, we are talking about someone who is supposed to know you. Somehow, y'all started talking about sweaters, and you mentioned you don't like sweaters because you hate fabric. Christmas comes, and they just happen to pull your name. They brought you a sweater that someone gave them, and they just re-gifted it. That's not putting a thought into your gift.

What if God just gave us anything, and it was something He knew we didn't want or like? We would be mad at God because He is supposed to know us.

I only asked Anthony to spend time with me two times throughout the year. That was my birthday and Valentine's Day. Not even our anniversary because that was Kayla's birthday, and it was about her. So, of course, I'm mad. Anthony had been calling my phone since I left. I turned my phone off. My sister and I enjoyed ourselves.

When we got back, Kayla and Ant were gone. So, he brought her back that morning. He was still mad at me. He just dropped her off and left and didn't want to talk. Kayla came in and hugged me. She said, "Hi Mama, I missed you." I told her I missed her too.

She says, "Look, Mama." She was showing me that she had a purple ribbon in her hair.

I said, "Aw, you look so cute."

She was six at this time, so she loved to talk. She said, "Do you know who put this in my hair?"

I said, "Your aunt, Shanell."

She said, "No."

I was like, "Who?"

She says, "My daddy's friend. I don't know her name."

Now, one thing about me: I don't play about my child.

And I don't like to put children in grown-ups' business. So, I'm just listening. She said, "We stayed over her house."

So, you know I'm heated. I asked her where was her dad. She said he was in the room with the lady.

Child, I got that phone. I called him. I said, "Why did you take my child over to some woman's house?" I told him he didn't have any respect for anybody. Of course, he denied everything. He said he didn't want to drive all the way home because he was drunk. He said that he slept on her couch. Now, when I go off, nobody is getting a word in. I exploded. This man has shown me time and time again that he didn't care about me, but I just kept on holding on to him, thinking he would change.

— *chapter* —

17

A RANDOM CALL

Weeks passed. I received a phone call from a random number. It was like 6:00 in the morning. I pick up; she says, "Hi, my name is Sandra. I just wanted to know what's the status of your and Anthony's relationship."

In my head, I was like, *oh Lord, here we go again. It's too early for this drama.* I'm like, *Lord, give me strength.* I told her we were married. She said Ant has been living with her ever since we moved out of our apartment. She said, "I was on the phone with him when you told him you were unhappy. Ant and I went to school together. We started out as friends. I was the one who told him to ask you about getting counseling."

I knew she was telling the truth because no one else was there when we discussed that.

She said, "He proposed to me." She started going on about their sex life and the things they were doing. All I could do was just shake my head. She said he told her we were getting a divorce, and this was the only reason she accepted his proposal.

This was the first time I had ever heard about us getting a divorce. It was hard to hear all this. We talked for about an hour that morning. She said, "You call every morning at the same time. He goes into the bathroom and talks to you. But this time, he left his phone in bed. So, when you called, I wrote down your number." She told me that the little white car he comes down there in was her car. "He tells me he has to come down there to spend time with his daughter."

She said he had filed for a divorce. She said she took him down there to file. This is what I mean about our motives. And the way we try to hurt the other woman. She already knew he filed for a divorce, so what was the purpose of her calling me and asking me the status of our marriage and all that other stuff? She knew that I would be hurt by this. She wanted me to know before I got the divorce papers.

He was already starting his new relationship lying and all wrong. I don't understand why men just can't be up-front with you. When they are not happy, why don't they say that? They just keep making you think everything is fine. I would rather for you to divorce me and move on than keep on lying and cheating on me.

I called Anthony. I said, "So, who is Sandra?"

He was like, "Man, don't call me with that. I'm trying to work. It's always something with you."

I said, "Yes, because of you." I told him that he was so stupid. I know that I had to really be mad using the word STUPID. I don't like that word. Going through all this stuff will make you come out of character. I never cussed him out. But did I want to? Now that is another book.

Ladies, notice that they are never the problem. This man put me through all this stuff. And said it's always something with me.

But see, this is very important. This is why a lot of women are in jail or prison. And not just women, men too. Because of all the pain.

The devil comes in when we are weak and gives us scripture that says an eye for an eye. Or do unto others. Or you reap what you sow. We have to be careful about using the word to justify our wrongdoing. The devil is tricky like that. He plays with our emotions.

I really didn't know what to do. I had no job, and I only had $87 that Ant gave me the day before. Ant took all the money out of our account. I'm living at my sister's house with a six-year-old child. I didn't know how to tell my family that I was getting a divorce.

Later that day I called and called. We argued. He hung up. We argued. He hung up. This went on for about two hours until Anthony got tired and said, "Since you want to act crazy. I am on my way to get the phone."

I said, "I don't care." I was talking BIG. I said, "I will have another by tomorrow."

How was I going to go get a new phone with no job and

no money? I guess that faith had to kick in somewhere because I let it out in the atmosphere.

Now I know y'all women are saying why did I give him that phone back? You should have just kept it and let him turn it off. Or just broke it up. I wasn't really thinking about any of that. It seemed like I was just numb.

Have you ever had a toothache, and the pain kept coming and coming? At first, the pain is unbearable, and it seems like you just want to pull your hair and every tooth out. Then you use everything to try to numb that tooth. Eventually, the pain subsides to the point where you can bear it for a while. Ladies, this is what we keep doing, numbing the pain and numbing the pain until we go to the dentist, and he says, "I'm sorry, it just can't be saved. You just got to get rid of it."

That's why it's important to follow the plan of God. When you don't follow the path of God, it seems like life is hard. This is why divorce rates are so high. Women are getting married for the wrong reasons. Just to say they have a husband or because their friends are doing it. Or for congratulations and validation from others. We are not doing it for love.

A lot of women have a problem with the word submit; this is only because we confuse submit with control. We say, "He's not going to control me." But if a man is loving you like you are supposed to be loved, it makes you yield to him. This is true love.

When we say love will make you do some crazy things,

it means like it's below zero, and you walk to the store and get her favorite snacks or something unusual, just like Jesus got on the cross for us. Not bust the windows out of his car or flatten his tires. That is another kind of crazy.

Anthony came and got the phone, but before he got the phone, Sandra had called back. The first time she called, she was talking nicely and calmly. Now she's yelling. Telling me to tell her fiancé to bring her car back. Y'all, this is what she is saying. "Carla, tell my fiancé to bring my car back."

He got the phone and left. I went upstairs and asked my sister, Lisa, if I could use her phone. She said, "Where is your phone?"

I said Anthony came and took it. She said, "Girl, you need a phone. Come on, I will get you a phone." I got my new phone, y'all. I made sure I called him and let him know (petty). He just hung up.

Late that night, or more like that morning, around 2:00 or 3:00, Jada called me. I was like, "What's up?"

She asked, "Who is Sandra?" I was trying to figure out how she knew Sandra. She said, "She's on Facebook with pictures of her and Ant. In one of the pictures, he is lying in her bed sleep. In the caption, she says, 'This is how a king is supposed to live, and she tagged him in it.'"

I'm like, "Oh girl, she ain't nobody."

So, I went to Facebook to see what Jada was talking about. Clear as day, there it was. Sandra even sent me a friend request. I was so embarrassed that I did not know what to do. I was like, *here we go again with the public embarrassment.* I was praying that none of my family members would see it.

We have to learn to be more transparent with our family, regardless of what it is. This is why so many women die. They either die from stress or from trying to hide everything from people. Or they are getting abused by their boyfriends or husbands.

When you look at the news and see a woman who was killed by her husband or boyfriend, when they interview the family member, they say he was a good boyfriend or husband. They did not see that coming because they hid everything to make their lives look good.

chapter

18

GETTING SERVED

My family and I were hanging out, just chilling because I was in pretend mode. But how was I going to tell them I was getting a divorce, even if we were close? So, we're playing, and suddenly the doorbell rings, so I answer it. It was my brother-in-law. Now, my brother-in-law is a sheriff, so when he came, I did not think anything. He would show up sometimes out of the blue.

We laughed, played, and kidded around. Then he said, "I need to talk to you." I'm looking like, *okay*. We went downstairs.

He was like, "I am here on a serious matter."

I said, "Okay."

He said, "Anthony has filed for a divorce."

I was like, "Okay," fighting the tears because it had gotten real.

He said, "I saw the address, and it looked familiar, so I

picked it up. I thought it would be better if I brought it to you."

In my head, I was like, *naw,* because I still didn't tell anybody at this point. It was embarrassing to me. But it was what it was. He went over all the documents with me. He asked me if I was okay. I said, "Yes," but was fighting tears left and right.

I could tell he was feeling some type of way, but this was all a part of his job. When he left, I went upstairs. Everybody was looking at me. So, I just came out with it. I said, "Anthony has filed for a divorce."

Everyone was just saying things to the point that I could not hear anybody. My sister Lisa said, "Girl, you are going to be alright; God got you." Y'all, tears rolled down my face so fast that everybody just started hugging me.

Believe it or not, it was a relief from the pressure. I don't know what I was expecting my family to say. This is what goes on in many households. We don't know how to tell anybody, so we pretend. We even try to stay in the relationship for our children. We must learn that our kids just want to be loved. It doesn't matter if the parents are together or not.

Two weeks before we had to go to court, Sandra and Anthony broke up. He calls and tells me he doesn't want a divorce. He said we could just get counseling. I said we will see.

The day before we had to go to court, he said, "You can just ride with me. I know you don't like to drive downtown."

Which was true, so I said, "That's fine."

Something told me not to hang up the phone. Ant was in the car with his cousin Doug. Doug said, "Cuz, I need you to take me over to some girl's house." I couldn't remember her name.

Ant says to him, "I need to go over somebody's house." He said a woman's name too but it wasn't clear.

I was like, "Okay." I hung up.

He noticed that his phone had lit up. So, he called me back. He said, "You heard us playing around?" He tried to act like he knew I was on the phone.

I said, "Yeah I heard everything."

He said, "Man, we were just playing around."

I was like, "Okay."

— chapter —

19

THE DIVORCE

A nthony came and picked me up so we could go to court. Yes, we rode together, but my dad used to always say, "Don't go anywhere without any money."

While entering court, Anthony was trying to convince me to get counseling. Y'all, I was really thinking about it so hard. I thought we could really work through this.

They called our name; we went into this room with a mediator. The mediator started asking us how we got to this point. So, I'm talking and crying because I have to relive it all over again, as though I'm in a movie. You really don't see yourself until you see yourself. The person that went through all that stuff was not me; I didn't feel like myself. Going through all this made it hard for me to be a great mom to my baby. No, I did not neglect her, I loved my child. It's just hard to give love properly when you're not getting it.

No, I'm not playing a victim; I'm just letting y'all know what comes along with the territory when you're not waiting on God. I don't care who you are or the amount of money you may have; if you're not with the right person, things are just not going to work out. Listen, in every relationship, there will be disagreements, even with the ones God designed for you. But there should also be a balance; the area I'm weak in, he should be strong in, and vice versa.

As we talked, I kept playing these events in my head. All I could hear was Pastor Robinson saying, "Carlo," that's what he used to call me because he couldn't say my name. He said, "You are a jewel; don't let no man treat you like you are not." I don't know why this was playing in my head over and over. God was giving me a way to escape, but I was still trying to fix it. I was like, *jewels have to be tried in the fire*, then I had to tell myself, *girl, if you don't shake it off.* So, when the mediator asked us what we wanted to do, I said, "I am tired. I have been through enough; I want a divorce."

We must make sure that we are not option two for these men. When things don't work in their favor, they try to come back to us. Anthony was mad. He said, "You know, we really could have worked on our marriage." *Why? So I can go back through the pain you caused me? No way.* I just could not do it. It was at that moment that I found myself and came to my senses.

Now I see how the prodigal son felt; he was about to eat the pig's slop. Like I said, you have to see yourself before you see yourself. He saw himself going out badly. I can only imagine him thinking, *how did I get from a palace to a pen?* Then he came to his senses. "I am royalty. I can just go back home; I don't have to be here."

This is what I had to tell myself: I am loved. But sometimes we forget that, especially when we have been going through something. You have family and friends that love you. Why are you putting yourself through this? Wait on God; God will send you a man who will love you despite your flaws.

We went into another room where the actual judge was. Anthony and I were talking; we even had moments where we laughed. The judge said, "Are y'all sure y'all want a divorce? Y'all are not like the other couples that come in here." She said, "They be cussing each other out. So are y'all sure?"

Anthony said, "I don't, but she does."

The Judge said, "Well, Mr. Hood, you just have to try and woo her back."

We laughed, then signed the divorce papers and left. I was about to get on the train to go home; Anthony said, "You don't have to do that; I will take you back home." The whole ride home was silent and awkward, but we made it home.

When I got home, Ant came in to speak to my mother; I could hear him telling her he tried to save our marriage. I forgot to tell y'all that my mother did not want us to get a divorce. She wanted us to work it out, but she didn't know all I had been through. I went into my sister's room; I was dancing, shouting, and praising God.

Y'all just don't know how the shackles were lifted off me. I felt free. No more fights. No more sleepless nights, and no more cheating. It was all over.

Anthony overheard me praising God. He came and told me he was about to go. He said I was acting different. I wasn't going to praise God in the courtroom, which is what I wanted to do. And I knew he wasn't happy about the decision, so I couldn't praise God with him, so I waited till I got home. The Bible says rejoice with them that rejoice. So that's what I did; I knew he wasn't going to understand.

Anthony and I were talking about how we were going to wait to let the pastor know that we had got a divorce; we were trying to figure out when and how. We went to church because we had another revival. Prophet Davis had come back. I was in the front of the church, and Anthony was in the back. Prophet Davis started preaching; He said, "Let me see the hands of married couples."

God has a way of doing things; when we are trying to figure it out, He's already in place setting it up. When he said, "Raise your hands," I did not raise my hand; he said, "Girl, raise your hand, you're married."

I'm whispering, "No, I'm not."

He said, "Weren't you married the last time I came?"

I was like, "Yes," giving him the side eye, like move on prophet. I could do him like that because we had that kind of friendship; every time he came, he would mess with me; he was a really cool man of God.

He walks to the back of the church and sees Anthony. He says, "There goes your husband."

I'm just looking like, *oh Lord, I'm embarrassed.* It doesn't take much for me to get embarrassed.

He asked Anthony where his wife was. Anthony points to the front at me. Now, the prophet is looking at me like I'm lying. The prophet said, "Why did you say you weren't married?"

I was like, "Because I'm not." Mind you, nobody in the church knew that we had got a divorce besides my family, so everyone looked at me as though I was lying. My sister Sheila is looking at Anthony like, *don't play with my sister.* So, after church, we had to explain our divorce to the prophet and the pastor.

CONCLUSION

God did not design marriage for divorce. When you experience a breakup or divorce, there is not really a way to handle it, but you can do so through the grace of God.

When you go through a breakup or divorce, it feels like your heart has stopped. You don't want to see or talk to anyone. You don't want to eat. There are sleepless nights. Sometimes, it makes you want to give up on life. Sometimes, it hurts so bad you just can't think straight.

Pain will cause you to do things you normally wouldn't do. Say, for instance, you are not a drinker; it will cause you to drink or go out more than usual. Sometimes, it causes you to be a social butterfly. You replace pain with people. You try to act like it did not harm you.

Divorce can cause you to neglect your personal hygiene, lose your faith in God, find comfort in food, or jump into another relationship quickly. These are just some of the symptoms I went through when experiencing my divorce. When I went through my divorce, like I said, I came home and rejoiced, but that was just one of the symptoms of trying to replace pain with people (my family).

When you have been with a person for 10 years, I can't lie, you miss that person. I thought about my child and how she was going to be affected by this. I had sleepless nights, and I turned to food as my comfort. I gained so much weight. Neglecting myself. Sometimes, I just stayed in bed and cried when everyone was asleep. I stopped going to church because I was mad at God. I did this for about a month and a half until God said, "That's enough. You are not going to keep blaming me for what you got yourself into." I knew He was right, and this time, I didn't argue. I had to take accountability for my actions. So, I had to get up and go back to church and face the music because, like I said, this was a small church, so there was no hiding. Everyone knew you and your business. But when I got there, I was greeted with so much love, which made it better.

Do we really think God doesn't know about relationships? He knows best. When God sends that man to us, and we get married, God still should be in that relationship with us. This is the only threesome you should have: GOD + HUSBAND + WIFE. If that husband seeks God first, God will tell that husband how to be intimate with you and how he should love you. God will also let that husband know that you are not happy in that relationship. And women, God will do the same for us, too, but we must put God first.

Bringing other people into your marriage is a sure way to failure. There are sayings in the streets, "If you're not getting it at home, get it somewhere else," or "What your husband or wife won't do, someone else will." Why get married? This brings on different spirits. The only orgies you should be having are (GOD + The Father + The Son + The Holy Spirit + husband + wife). God will show you how to be pleasing to your husband. Hebrews 13:4 says the bed is undefiled. God created sex for marriage; it's supposed to be pure and intimate, something you have never experienced before, just like having your first newborn baby. When you have sex before marriage, it causes you to compare your sexual experiences that you have had with other men with your husband. Now you have created thoughts in your head that he is not doing this like this one, and he is not doing that like the other one. It causes you to miss what you have already experienced. You cannot miss what you did not experience.

We have so many people cheating in marriages, and divorce rates are high because that husband or wife is looking for that which they once had. So, they will sleep with this one and that one until that flesh is satisfied. In a marriage, you may have disagreements, but when you are with the right mate, you can talk about anything. Communication is the key, but God is first.

The god of this world (the devil) is blinding our minds, and he will have us thinking that anything is acceptable with marriage. That's why we have same-sex marriages and transgender marriages. In some states, you can even marry yourself and even animals. All kinds of stuff.

So, with that being said, seek God in ALL your ways, and He will direct your path. Don't leave home without Him. Don't get married without God or do anything without Him.